A GUIDE TO EFFECTIVE WORSHIP LEADING

by Michael A. Strickland

A GUIDE TO EFFECTIVE WORSHIP LEADING

This manual provides practical tools that worship leaders and teams can use as they lead congregations into the presence of God.

Michael A. Strickland Ministries
Atlanta, Georgia

www.mastrickland.com

Published by MAStrickland Enterprise
111 Kelleytown Road; McDonough, Ga. 30252

Strickland, Michael A 1968–

A Guide to Effective Worship Leading
ISBN 978-1-7374422-0-2

Editor, Maureen Conley
Book Production, Dawn James/Publish and Promote

Printed in the United States of America.

CONTENTS

ACKNOWLEDGMENTS

Thanks to everyone who has been a part of my life and has encouraged me to write this manual for worship leaders and teams. After 30 years of working and serving in the music industry, I have learned a lot! I appreciate the prophetic impartations spoken over my life that encouraged me to write this manual.

Mt. Olive Baptist Church – the place where it all began. There, I spent my formative years: the ones when we used to have a choir for every Sunday of the month. First Sunday was the Mass, Second Sunday was the Senior Choir, Third Sunday was the Youth Choir, and Fourth Sunday was the Male Choir. I appreciate these choirs because they helped me develop and mature as a musician.

Friendship Baptist Church, College Park, Ga. – the place where I stretched my wings and served as the Minister of Music.

Little Bethel Baptist Church – my genesis church in Mableton, where I pastored 12+ people. It was with this outstanding group of individuals that I became aware that God's plan for my life was to become worship. So, it is my honor to acknowledge that body of believers and thank God for the times we shared because those times shaped me.

Victory Tabernacle Church International – the place where I serve as Chief Worship Leader. God, in all His sovereignty, allows me to share worship with this awesome community of believers. Weekly, we get the opportunity to ascend to the "City of the Living God" (Hebrews 12:22–24) and experience a fresh encounter. I appreciate every person who attends and serves with me.

You – Thanks for investing in your ministry and endeavoring to use the practical tools that are inside this guide to create an atmosphere where God's presence and power can be revealed. To all the teams and ministries that I have shared these practical tools with already, thank you!

It is my prayer, as individuals gather in their respective sanctuaries and churches, we seek the presence of God more than any other presence. If you feel that this manual will provide tools that will help you, then turn the pages and let's grow together!!

INTRODUCTION

The 100th division of the Psalms is an invitation for all to enter into the sacred presence of God with unbridled joy and hearts filled with thanksgiving. At the point of our entrance, we should have with us the expectation that His presence will accompany us as we ascend. We should expect to be meeting with our God, touching Him, and sensing Him touching us back. The psalm speaks to why we should adopt this posture: "God has made us His own people; God has created us; God chose us and loved us."

The Bible records historical examples where the people praised and worshipped God, and then supernatural things began to happen:

- 2 Chronicles 5:12–14 ~ The presence of God took possession of the temple, halting the work of the astounded priests.

- Joshua 6:5 ~ Under God's direction, the walls came down.

- 2 Chronicles 20:22 ~ Hearing the people's praise, God set an ambush for their enemies.

In our times together as the body of Christ, it is important that we recognize that, in each opportunity we are given to gather, it is the glory of God that we seek. Moses says in Exodus 33:15 MSG "If your presence doesn't take the lead here, call this trip off right now." The glory of God is His manifest presence. His presence changes the atmosphere. His presence gives us the opportunity to touch Him in a way that will change our current situation. As we ascend in our worship encounters, we must realize that the spirit of God must accompany us. In His presence there is fullness of joy (Psalm 16:11 KJV).

I want to share from my experiences some of the changes that I have seen take place in the church, including how we've gone from devotion to praise and worship, when we should instead be cultivating an atmosphere in which the presence of God is felt and lives are changed.

In this manual, I want to share lessons that I've learned as a musician turned pastor/chief worship leader. They have caused me to experience God in ways that are both fresh and relevant.

I want to share moments during my development as worship leader when I did things right and times when I made mistakes along the way. So, let's journey together and raise our expectations of the times together when we get the privilege to worship our God.

Consider

- Worship is both an attitude and an act. When we sing "Give thanks with a grateful heart" … it's about an attitude!
- Authentic/true worship takes place on the inside, in the heart or spirit of the worshipper (Psalm 45:1; 103:1–2).
- Worship pleasing to God must be unfeigned and transparent, offered with a humble and pure heart (Psalm 24:3–4; Isaiah 66:2).
- Worship must be done because God is God and you love Him just because.
- Worship exudes from the very fabric of our being.
- It is a lifestyle that we embrace and live daily.

CHAPTER ONE:
BE INVITATIONAL

THEME: ENCOURAGE, DON'T BADGER.

Our first goal in effective worship leading should be to fill the worship encounter with a sense of invitation, not threat. I have discovered that oftentimes when worship leaders lead, they hurl commands at the participants instead of graciously extending invitations. Commands make us feel we're being forced to participate in the worship experience, whereas invitations suggest we're being welcomed to unite and experience God for our own sake. So, it is vitally important that, as worship leaders, we establish an atmosphere that is inviting and welcoming. We don't want to create puppets who just respond to our commands automatically, so-called fifth responders (those who need the leader to utter different commands before they actively engage in the service). The danger in creating fifth responders is that the worship leader, too, will be programmed to respond in certain ways, based on the responders' response. If the responders fail to respond, the leader is likely to step into a badgering stance instead of a welcoming one.

Scripture speaks

Psalm 34:3 KJV~ *Oh, magnify the Lord with me and* ***let us*** *exalt His name together...*
Psalm 122:1 KJV~ *I was glad when they said unto me,* ***let us*** *go into...*
Micah 4:2 KJV~ *Come and* ***let us*** *go up to the mountain of the Lord...*
Psalm 95:6 KJV ~ *Oh come,* ***let us*** *worship and bow down...*

Transparent moment

I vividly remember leading worship and finding the people uninterested and not responsive. I immediately began to badger and beg them, to spew words meant to make them feel bad about not responding, to browbeat them until I "loosened them up," as I called it. I used phrases that were familiar to worshippers in many circles, ones I thought were helping but that felt cutting and hurtful to the participants.

Phrases to avoid:

- *Come on, saints, get with it.*
- *Come on y'all, wake up.*
- *God ain't done nothing for nobody but me?*
- *You can't think of one thing that God has done just this week that will make you give Him a praise?*
- *Clap your hands like you really mean it, and don't patty-cake with God.*
- *If you didn't come to praise Him, then you might as well leave.*
- *We don't have time to be sitting here wasting time doing nothing.*
- *What you come for?*
- *If you didn't come to praise Him, then what you come for?*

- *Don't be looking at me like you mad and been sucking on lemons all night.*
- *Why you wasting your time for two hours if you are not going to praise God?*
- *Why did you get out of bed, get dressed and make up your face to look pretty if you are not going to praise God?*

I mimicked what I had heard others say as they led worship. It was a popular but ineffective method. My imitating was doing more harm than good, because I sounded cantankerous and made the atmosphere much less conducive to worship. Yet I was so sure that I was being effective! I had heard and seen these techniques demonstrated in almost every church or setting I found myself in. I felt they were appropriate because people who were close to me applauded my efforts and understood my position as they supported me. Little did I know that I was doing harm. Following a popular leader doesn't automatically mean that you are leading people in an effective way.

Lesson learned: It is important that we shape our phrases as invitational questions and not as commands. The worship leader's role is to make the corporate body feel the desire, while an electrifying atmosphere is set, to join in and receive from the Lord. The leader is to lead the house into worship, not force the people to go. As the worship leader, you must be so infused with the power of God residing in you that it emanates from you and attracts others.

Invitational phrases include:

- *Let us go up.*
- *Let us ascend.*
- *Let us make a joyful noise unto the Lord.*
- *Will you bless the Lord with me?*
- *Will you magnify the Lord?*
- *Will you join me as we ascend in our worship?*

- *Want you unite with me as we release a sound in this atmosphere?*
- *Want you clap your hands and shout unto God with a voice of triumph?*
- *Want you lift your hands in the sanctuary?*
- *Can we unite and release a sound?*
- *Can we use our voices to lift up the name of Jesus?*
- *Can we choose to rejoice and be glad on today?*
- *Can we magnify, exalt, lift up, make large,*
  express our gratitude to God today?
- *Is anybody grateful in the house today?*
- *Will somebody help me lift Him up?*
- *Will somebody join us as we express our love for God?*
- *Shall we enter into the sacred space where the enemy cannot dwell?*
- *Shall we lift our voices and magnify the Lord together?*

Using these kinds of phrases signifies that it's not just a performance you want; it's not just the leader's actions that matter; it's not just for your own benefit that you are speaking; it's not for the participant to just sit back and wait, watch and grow weary, and yet it's not a seat in hell if the participant doesn't respond; and it doesn't make the participant a bad person for choosing not to participate. Instead, the invitational approach suggests that you have tasted something good, and you are inviting the participant to do the same. Once the leader can grasp the essence and importance of invitational phrases and use them effectively, the worshipper will gladly enter into the presence of the almighty God.

It is appropriate and recommended that you use Scripture as you lead worship. The Word of God is the source of life. We declare and decree truth through the Word, and it is performed as we worship. In John 17:17, Jesus declares that His Word is truth, and if we use truth in the worship encounter, we do not have to make up our own words and phrases to use.

- *I was glad when they said unto me, let us go into the house of the Lord.* (Psalm 122:1 KJV)
- *Lift up your heads, O ye gates: and be ye lift up, ye everlasting doors: and the King of glory shall come in...* (Psalm 24:7 KJV)
- *Oh magnify the Lord with me, and let us exalt His name together.* (Psalm 34:3 KJV)
- *O Clap your hands, all ye people: shout unto God with a voice of triumph.* (Psalm 47:1 KJV)
- *And we know that all things work together for good...* (Romans 8:28 KJV)
- *Bless the Lord, O my soul: and all that is within me...* (Psalm 103:1 KJV)
- *Father, I thank thee that thou hast heard me... And I know that thou hearest me always.* (John 11:41–42 KJV)
- *Lord. You are my Shepherd and I shall not want.* (Psalm 23:1 KJV)
- *Father you are from everlasting to everlasting.* (Psalm 90:2 KJV)

Wise word #1

The excerpts from the Word of God that you use should speak to the atmosphere that you have set (or intend to set) as you lead. Please correlate the Word and songs. David declares in Psalm 138:2 KJV *I* As worship leaders, we must understand that it is not our riffs, runs, or special effects that transform the lives of the people, it is the Word of God.

Wise word #2: Connections cause sparks

As an illustration, I want to talk about the jumper cables used to jump-start the dead battery in a car. The cables alone don't have sufficient power to start the battery; they must be connected to a power source. Once the cables are connected, they send out sparks, indicating that power is flowing through them and they can do what they were designed to do.

So it is with worship. God is the power source. The worship leader serves as one end of the cable, and the congregation as the other end of the cable. As the worship leader invites and the people respond, sparks ignite a presence that shifts an atmosphere and invites the presence of God to be free in the encounter.

Wise word #3

The purpose of the corporate gathering is to ascend in our worship unto God. David asks the question in Psalm 24, who can possibly ascend to the mountain of God? Who can stand before Him in sacred spaces? This suggests to us that our worship must "go up" where God is. So, it is vital that the worship leader extend an invitation to experience God.

My takeaways

Tools that I will use

Notes

CHAPTER TWO:

SYNCHRONIZE LEADERSHIP

THEME: THE CHIEF WORSHIP LEADER AND THE DESIGNEE MUST BE IN SYNC.

Sync ~ to sense what is unspoken but transmitted through the Spirit of God, orchestrating our time together. It is the art of communicating so that individuals move in parallel in a forward processional, without warning or prior notification. It's having a connection to, and a listening ear for, the Spirit of God. It's the chief worship leader knowing when to press, lift, push, and release.

Press: To "press" is to move into the anointing that is present and God, to discern music and prophetic songs that have never been heard or ministered before. It is the ability to sing unto God a new song. It is the ability to sense, hear, and obey God in the moment and sing what you hear the Lord saying.

Lift: To "lift" suggests that we understand when the Grace and Glory have left the current ministry moment. It is recognizing God's timing as we flow through the encounter together. It is knowing when to move on and end or change songs to go deeper into the worship moment.

Push: To "push" suggests plowing the atmosphere so that the Glory can fill and control. Oftentimes as we minister, we may find ourselves struggling with a hard energy. To overcome it, the worship leader must cultivate the soil so that the incorruptible seed of the Word of God may be planted in the soil of the participants' hearts.

Release: Needing to "release" indicates that you have "milked" the song to the point of ineffectiveness. At this stage, it is not necessary to try and make something happen.

Sync and link

As worship leader, you are to submit to the chief worshipper's authority in the house where you are serving. It is not proper to attempt to lead in the current house the way you have led in another house of worship.

Understand that God speaks to each of us individually. We should all honor that individual vision in every worship leader. But when God appoints you to carry out another's vision, it is your responsibility to embrace the culture and climate of the set Man or Woman of God.

The Man or Woman of God who has been assigned as leader of the house is the chief worship leader. That person sets the tone for the sound and flow of the Spirit in the atmosphere. God speaks to the chief as He did to Moses. It is the chief's responsibility to set the tone and the worship leader's responsibility to embrace the tone to execute the sound. It is vitally important that the two are in sync with each other, just like a hand and glove.

Suggested ways the two can sync:

- There should be conversational moments where the chief and leader get acquainted.
- The desired goal for the house should be established.
- The worship leader should have a conversation with the chief leader to solidify boundaries for worship.
- The worship leader should submit completely to the authority or set person of the house.
- The worship leader should incline their ear to hear the cultural sound.
- The worship leader could study the chief leader's mannerisms.
- The chief should, at times, allow the leader to be completely in charge of the encounter, to encourage connection.
- Both should remain in prayer as the sound elevates and as the Spirit of God speaks and be willing to create an atmosphere suitable for various generations.
- The chief worship leader must trust the worship leader to flow in the vein that God has instructed the chief worshipper to flow in.
- The worship leader must yield, be flexible, and adjust as the Spirit of God moves in the worship experience.

Transparent moment

As chief worship leader, I value loyalty and relationships. It is very important to me that I build a relationship first with the worship leader and that we are loyal one to another. The chief has to work on trust, the fear of rejection, and maturation. As chief leader, my view is that there is no competition between but a completion thereof.

My father was my senior pastor for 39 years and, as his musician for 24 years, I heard God speak to me, but it wasn't my position to lead but to be loyal to the chief while serving.

God wants...

Ephesians 4:16 AMPCE ~ *From Him the whole body (the church, in all its various parts), joined and knitted firmly together by what every joint supplies, when each part is working properly, causes the body to grow up in (unselfish) love.*

We can expect to see growth when the joints are locked in place and synced together. Each joint fits together by what it supplies to the other joint. The unifying power of synchronization yields visitations from heaven. I believe God desires the chief and the leader to supply one to another and grow the body of Christ.

MY TAKEAWAYS

TOOLS THAT I WILL USE

Notes

CHAPTER THREE:

FEEL TO FILL

THEME: FEEL THE ROOM FOR HIS PRESENCE TO FILL THE ROOM.

The ultimate goal of each encounter is that the presence of God be experienced. Moses says in Exodus 33:15 KJV, as God instructs him to lead the people, "If your presence doesn't go with us, carry us NOT up hence." In other words, if it's not God's presence leading us forward, then we need not move. Moses's perspective should be the same perspective that worship leaders hold during every opportunity they are given to lead others into God's presence. The worship leader should not make a move alone or solely with the people present. The presence of God should always *accompany*, as the atmosphere is set for a divine move of God.

As a worship leader leads the people into the presence of God, the atmosphere is very important. A worship leader needs to consider the culture of the house while planning the set and implementing it. The sound of the house should be a key factor in preparing for the encounter that is to take place. The feel of the house and the room in each encounter is going to be different because of God's intention for the moment and the individuals that have gathered.

What do we mean by "culture" in the context of ministry?

"Culture" is the overarching way an organization does things, the atmosphere of the house. This is the music ministry that people will respond to even if you minister the same songs weekly. There is a sound that each house carries that invites congregants to participate without being asked or prompted. It is that sound that speaks to the essence of the house's theological perspective on God. For example:

1. If people's perspective on God is one in which *He* is the focal point of their existence, then whenever they hear songs that speak to the character of God, they will have an automatic response. Every time they hear the worship leaders minister about God, they will respond.

2. If a people's experience of God speaks to struggle, then when they hear songs that speak to struggle, they will automatically respond because that's how they have studied and experienced God.

As worship leader, it is imperative you factor the culture into every encounter.

Traditional cultures: In these cultures, leading worship requires the leader to sing songs that are more traditional and rooted in the culture of the people, so that the feel of the room is conducive to the power being felt. If contemporary songs are occasionally desired so that the music will speak to all generations, they have to be introduced gradually and tried and tested before they can be successfully repeated.

Contemporary cultures: In these cultures, leading worship requires the leader to sing nontraditional songs. Traditional songs will seem out of place and out of date because the atmosphere speaks to the contemporary and suits more popular songs. Artists whose songs are in popular rotation at the time will be those whose songs are heard the most in any worship experience. Introducing a traditional song has to be gently explored and cautiously done.

Combo cultures: These are the cultures where a variety of genres will be heard and experienced in the encounter. This is usually a multigenerational congregation where everyone will receive worship that speaks to their generation, and no one will feel or seem out of place or reject what is being experienced. In these cultures, you will hear hymns, *capella* songs, foot stomping, tambourine playing, guitar, string instruments, and a combination of all genres. In a combo-culture atmosphere, these sounds will be welcomed because the multiple generations embrace the message and don't simply focus on rhythm and beat.

As worship leaders, even though plans may have been made for a set, we must always be sensitive to the culture of the house and the feel of the room and then be in position to make proper adjustments if God's presence is to fill the room. There is nothing worse than to sense God doing something in an atmosphere and then force a prepared set of songs that doesn't flow with the movement at that moment.

Worship-leading in a Multigenerational Ministry

I absolutely love the environments in which the worship leader leads in a multigenerational ministry, because of the type of ministry this practice offers. However, the leader has to be sensitive and skilled to know when and how to effectively minister to the people. The styles and genres of music should be ministered in an authentic way so that each generation can receive and appreciate the ministry. If a worship leader is ministering a hymn of the church, there is no need for riffs and runs and vocal show-offs. The worship leader should stay with the character of the style and respect and honor it. It is important that the worship leader speak the musical language of the church in which they serve.

Worship in a multicultural ministry

This is the ultimate atmosphere to worship in because it allows us the opportunity to grow into worship leaders who can be effective no matter what environment we find ourselves in. It is important to be well-rounded as a worship leader so that you can be effective when ministering to various congregations and crowds. We must be mindful that God loves the world and not just one particular culture.

Transparent moment

As a worship leader who is multigenerational in repertoire, it is an effort for me not to incorporate all my multigenerational music in all my encounters as worship leader. I feel that every generation should be able to relate to and participate in the worship encounter every time we gather.

My takeaways

Tools that I will use

Notes

CHAPTER FOUR:

CALL HIM BY HIS NAME

THEME: USE THE NAMES OF GOD AS YOU ASCEND TO THE CITY.

Ascend: to go up; to meet; to go over; to go up over; to bring up; to draw up; to be led up; to be taken up into.

It is the worship leader's assignment to lead the congregation to ascend to the city where the living God resides. Although it is not a physical place, it is a spiritual realm where we draw nigh unto God's presence and join the angels' invisible celebration and the great cloud of witnesses.

The vehicle that the worship leader uses is the names and characters of God.

When we set the atmosphere right by using the names of God, the people know who we've come to celebrate, they know the guest of honor, they know who is the center of attention, they know why we should be engaged, they begin to feel strength in the room, they are invited to refocus and redirect their postures and positions, they have no room for doubt as to our agenda. The people will be empowered to take the focus off their current situations and release their faith for their future expectations.

Not only do we use the names, but we should use the characteristic of each name as we worship. The invitation is to ascend and allow others to share in His names' ability. We should elaborate on the function and character of His name as we lead the people into His presence.

Elohim means "God" ~ This name refers to God's incredible power and might. He is the One and Only God. He is Supreme. He is the One on whom we can fully rely. He is Sovereign. He is the One we can completely trust. He is the Mighty One over all of nature. He is our Creator God. He is the source of our very being… God.

Yahweh means "The Lord" ~ Yahweh is derived from the Hebrew word for "I AM." It is the proper name of the divine person, coming from the verb that means "to exist," "to be." It is a name of authority.

I am Alpha and Omega
I am the first and the last
I am the bread of life
I am the God who heals thee
I am the God who protects thee
I am the God who provides for thee
I am the Great I am
I am God...

Whenever the worship leader begins and ends with God, a life transformation must take place. Leading from this place takes the pressure off the leader and places it on God to manifest among the people who are present. If the focus is on the worship leader, then the leader has to show up and perform, but if the focus is on God, then God is obligated to show up and move on behalf of the people.

El Shaddai means "God Almighty" ~ God's name, El Shaddai, reminds us that He is all-powerful, He is the Mighty One. He is strong and is our strength, He is all-sufficient. He is more than sufficient to meet any need. He is power and provision. He takes my weaknesses and provides me with strength.

> *Genesis 17:1 KJV ~ And when Abram was ninety years old and nine, the LORD appeared to Abram, and said unto him, I am the Almighty God; walk before me, and be thou perfect.*

> *Genesis 35:11 KJV ~ And God said unto him, I am God Almighty: be fruitful and multiply; a nation and a company of nations shall be of thee, and kings shall come out of thy loins.*

Jehovah Rapha means the "God who Heals" ~ He is the great physician. He heals our entire being. He is the God who.

> *Exodus 15:26 KJV ~ And said, If thou wilt diligently hearken to the voice of the LORD thy God, and wilt do that which is right in his sight, and wilt give ear to his commandments, and keep all his statutes, I will put none of these diseases upon thee, which I have brought upon the Egyptians: for I am the LORD that healeth thee.*

Jehovah Shalom means "The Lord is my Peace" God reveals himself as peace.

> *Judges 6:24 KJV ~ Then Gideon built an altar there unto the LORD, and called it Jehovahshalom: unto this day it is yet in Ophrah of the Abiezrites.*

Jehovah Rahi means "The Lord is my Shepherd" ~ He feeds me. He leads me to pastures. He is my friend who.

> *Ezekiel 34:11–15 KJV ~ For thus saith the Lord GOD; Behold, I, even I, will both search my sheep, and seek them out. As a Shepherd seeketh out his flock in the day that he is among his sheep that are scattered; so will I seek out my sheep, and will deliver them out of all places where they have been scattered in the cloudy and dark day. And I will bring them out from the people, and gather them from the countries, and will bring them to their own land, and feed them upon the mountains of Israel by the rivers, and in all the inhabited places of the country. I will feed them in a good pasture, and upon the high mountains of Israel shall their fold be: there shall they lie in a good fold, and in a fat pasture shall they feed upon the mountains of Israel. I will feed my flock, and I will cause them to lie down, saith the Lord GOD.*

There are more names and characteristics of God that the worship leader can use. The leader must apply the name and character that befits the atmosphere and the flow in the worship experience.

Transparent moment

I began using the names and characteristics of God before I understood and had full proof that He could be in my life the person described by the name. I was, again, mimicking what I had seen and heard until sickness hit my physical body and I could testify that God is Jehovah Rapha.

It was in July 2004 that I suffered blood clots (DVT) after having my legs straightened. After my surgery I began to recover, but during physical therapy blood clots formed in my legs and lungs. To deal with the excruciating pain, I would have to do the one-less-pillow move to lie flat (that is, starting with pillows behind me, I had to remove them one at a time to get down to the next pillow). When I first arrived at the hospital, the doctors said they were amazed I was still living because of the depth of the clot in my lungs. I was rolled into a room at 5 a.m. on a Sunday. I spent a week on heparin (which thins the blood) waiting for my blood to thin enough to make it safe for me to be released.

It was the following Saturday that I looked at my wife and told her that I was healed and that I was going home the next morning. It was 5 a.m., seven days after I arrived, that the nurse walked into my room and I said to her, "This is the reading we've been waiting for. God has healed me." When she came back, she informed me that I was going to be released that day.

I testify because God moved me from regimen to revelation: He is a healer. I started saying it before I had the authority to say it, but I did it anyway. Since my recovery, I know that God is a healer.

As the chief worshipper, I stand boldly now and declare with full proof that Jehovah Rapha is a healer because I have experienced Him to be just that ~ my HEALER! Hallelujah!

Sample Openings to Use the Names and Character of God

#1 ~ Father, we've entered into your gates with thanksgiving, and we've gotten to the courts, and there is a praise that's about to come out of our mouths. We assemble to honor and recognize you as Jehovah Jireh ~ the Lord God who provides. We thank you today because you have been provisions on Monday when we needed strength; Tuesday when we needed courage; Wednesday when we needed more grace; Thursday when we were out of resources; Friday when my relationships were rocky; Saturday when my focus was almost gone. And so, we come today to thank you for being Jehovah Jireh, our provider. We thank you today for being Elohim ~ God. There is none before you, none besides you and none after you. You are Supreme God, and you do whatever you want to do, however you want it done. We gather to give you thanks because you are our Shepherd and we shall not want. Thank you for being our everything.

#2 ~ Father, we thank you for this is the day that you have made, and we choose to rejoice and be glad in it. We thank you for being Jehovah Shalom, the God of peace. Your Word says if we keep our minds stayed on you, that you will keep us in perfect peace. And Lord, this week, we thank you for peace in our homes, peace on our jobs, peace in our marriages, peace in our families, peace in the midst of confusion. Thank you, Lord, that it was the kind of peace that surpasses all understanding. When I didn't know which way to go and what road to take, your peace settled me. When I couldn't trace your hand, I had to trust your heart; it was your peace that calmed me. Father, your peace has guarded our hearts and minds through Christ Jesus. Father, I wanna thank you for your everlasting peace at all times, in every way.

My takeaways

Tools that I will use

Notes

CHAPTER FIVE:

MY GETHSEMANE

THEME: THE GETHSEMANE EXPERIENCE IS NEEDED AND WORTHWHILE.

JESUS IN THE GARDEN (MATTHEW 26:36–46)

The garden at Gethsemane, a place whose name literally means "oil press," is located on a slope of the Mount of Olives just across the Kidron Valley from Jerusalem. A garden of ancient olive trees stands there to this day. Jesus frequently went to Gethsemane with His disciples to pray. Jesus's despair in the Garden was so deep that the Bible records that in His agony, His sweat was, as it were, great drops of blood falling to the ground (Luke 22:44 KJV). The image illustrates how difficult it is to be in a season of life where your destiny requires pressing for the oil to flow—and yet now necessary it is, too.

Jesus experienced some shifts that, I want to point out, make a worship leader anointed (what we call "oily").

He prayed

Matthew 26:36 MSG ~ Then Jesus went with them to a garden called Gethsemane, and told His disciples, "Stat here while I go over there to pray."

As the worship leader leads others into the presence of God, the leader must have a strong prayer life and a strong connection with God to lead the congregation to their own connection with God. A worship leader who doesn't pray is like a car without a motor.

Scripture teaches us that God hears us, God responds to us, and God commands us to pray. Throughout the Word of God, we discover that God gives us a posture (prayer) to assume, and He remains readily available to respond to us. In 2 Chronicles 7:14, God says that if His people pray, He will heal them. In 1 Thessalonians 5:16–18, God says it is His will that His people pray without ceasing. In Ephesians 6:18, God says we should pray in the Spirit on all occasions with all kinds of requests. In Jeremiah 29:12, God says we should pray to Him and He will listen. In Proverbs 15:8, God says that the prayer of the upright pleases Him. In Romans 12:12 God says to be faithful in prayer. In Luke 18:1, God says we ought to always pray and never give up.

When the worship leader has a personal prayer life, it will be evident in public life. In other words, what is done in secret will be revealed in the open.

Let your oil do the work

It is not the worship leader's responsibility to make or force a move of God in our encounters. If it is God's time to be together with us, we must trust that God has the power to know what is expected in those moments. It is our responsibility to serve as an usher and invite people to ascend to the city of God (Hebrews 12:22).

The more time we spend with God when we are in front of His people, the more we will be filled with His presence when we are in the presence of His people.

The worship leader must spend countless hours with God and know the working power of His love in their own life so that the shadow of His presence can fill the temple of worship and lives can be transformed. In Acts 5:15, Peter's shadow was so anointed that people were healed and delivered. When the worship leader experiences a Gethsemane, the anointing in their life will permeate the encounter and people will be healed, delivered, and set free.

The worship leader has to love God so much that their heart speaks to Him first when they lead and not to the people who have gathered. The worship leader's first worship presence is God's presence. The first person the worship leader desires to be with is God. The only person that the leader seeks to please is God. The worship leader has an audience of One and that One is God.

He parted ways

Matthew 26:39, 42, 44 MSG

Going a little ahead... praying (v. 39)

He then left them a second time and prayed (v. 42)

<u>And went back a third time to pray</u> (v. 44)

As worship leader, it is important to endure the season of separation from things and people who are not ready to take advantage of being in the presence of God. When Jesus visited the home of Mary and Martha, the custom was to make a guest in your home as welcome as possible. So, Martha busied herself doing what she and Mary traditionally did, but Mary broke with tradition and sat at Jesus's feet. Martha then asked Jesus to tell Mary to get up and help, but Jesus said that Mary had made a better choice. Jesus meant that it was wiser to sit at His feet than to remain with ordinary things and people.

Sometimes you have to go it alone

In Genesis 13:14, God speaks to Abram after he parted ways with Lot and said to him to lift up his eyes in all directions from the place where he was, because another dimension was being revealed in his life. Similarly, as the worship leader parts ways with others in the process of being anointed by God, the leader will be prepared to experience the next level of anointing that God intends. Reminder to the leader: Everyone cannot go into the sacred space you are bound for, *so part ways*.

He prostrated Himself

I believe that when one lies prostrate before God, it signifies humility and the utmost reverence to God. Although many postures may be used, the prostrate posture forces one to focus on God alone. Jesus demonstrates this posture for us in the Garden of Gethsemane.

Matthew 26:39 MSG~ ... and fell on his face, praying

Sometimes you must let yourself be crushed

Breaking points in the worship leader's life are designed to bless the people because in those times of trouble, oil is poured over your life. The worship leader must lie prostrate before the Lord God and desire a sincere crushing of the things hindering their effectiveness as a worship leader. Because the leader stands before the people physically, what's inside them stands as well. Realize that unhealed wounds in the life of the worship leader may bleed. All worshippers must ask, as David did in Psalm 51, that God have mercy upon them, that He blot out their iniquities, wash away their transgressions, correct their bad habits, cleanse them of their sins, restore unto them the joy of God's salvation, create in them a clean heart, and bless them by renewing within their leader the right spirit.

Scripture speaks...

Numbers 20:16 KJV ~ And Moses and Aaron went from the presence of the assembly unto the door of the tabernacle of the congregation, and they fell upon their faces: and the glory of the Lord appeared unto them.

1 Chronicles 29:20 KJV ~ And David said to all the congregation, Now bless the Lord your God. And all the congregation blessed the Lord God of their fathers, and bowed down their heads, and worshipped the Lord, and the king.

Genesis 17:3 KJV ~ And Abram fell on his face: and God talked with him.

Nehemiah 8:6 KJV ~ And Ezra blessed the Lord, the great God. And all the people answered, Amen, Amen, with lifting up their hands: and they bowed their heads, and worshipped the Lord with their faces to the ground.

Luke 5:12 KJV ~ And it came to pass, when he was in a certain city, behold a man full of leprosy: who, seeing Jesus, fell on his face, and besought him, saying, Lord, if thou wilt, thou canst make me clean.

The worship leader must be crushed for the oil the of God to flow in and through their life.

Transparent moment

My first pastorate was at the Little Bethel Baptist Church, Mableton Georgia, where the membership was about fifteen people on a good Sunday and five of the fifteen were my immediate family. I served there for four years as senior pastor. During my tenure there, God began to have me deal with some areas in my life that I need to crush so that the anointing oil would flow out of my life. I realized that if I was going to be a worshipper, I had to deal with some issues in my life.

I dealt with my childhood trauma.

As a child there were several events in my life that left a wound I failed to heal from the inside out. It developed a scar, but the wound still festered. I found I'd become bitter because of the things that had happened, and unforgiveness was dwelling in my heart (permanently, I had decided). I was never going to forgive the people or the circumstances in my life, I thought, but then I discovered that if I did not deal with the trauma, its impact was going to persist.

In all these areas, I prayed, cried, departed, and laid prostrate on the altar, allowing God to help me deal with my pain as I was being crushed for His glory. I used as my focal Scripture Romans 8:18, where Paul said, "*For I reckon that the sufferings of this present time are not worthy to be compared with the glory which shall be revealed in us.*" I knew that if the glory of God was going to be revealed, I would need to deal with the things that were causing me to suffer. Otherwise, I would be leading from a place of hurt and viewing life through a dysfunctional lens. At the time, I'd only mastered the art of performing for a response—and I was good at it.

Lesson learned: Never lead for a response from the people, because when the people do not respond, you will take it personally, *thinking they are rejecting you as leader.*

My takeaways

Tools that I will use

Notes

CHAPTER SIX:

SONG MEDLEYS

THEME: PLAN YOUR SETS PRAYERFULLY.

As we discussed in chapter 2, the worship leader must spend time in prayer seeking guidance and direction from God on how to plan and prepare for the worship encounter, to align with the chief worship leader's vision for the set time. When putting together song sets, as we call them, I urge all worship leaders to pray and ask God to show them the faces of the people who will be attending the encounter. The worship leader's assignment is to initiate, with the people who will be attending the encounter, the ascension process to the city of the living God.

It is very important that the worship leader align with the chief worship leader to impact the lives of the worshippers. I believe God will show the worship leader the faces of the people who will need to be ministered to and that He will also place an urgency in the heart of the worship so that the leader worships in a manner that speaks to the requests of the individuals gathered. So, it is paramount that the worship leader pray and ask God for His direction and guidance. It is very important for the worship leader to build a medley while keeping the worshippers in mind. The leader should not put a set of songs together for the sake of filling time; instead, once song sets are organized, listeners should be left with the melody or some part of the song in their hearts so they can participate when the songs are ministered in future encounters.

New material and song introduction

A rule of worship is to present songs that will speak to the congregation being led into worship. The worship leader monitors and tracks the weekly encounters to build on each week's song selection. As new songs are introduced, the worship leader must have the goal of embedding each song and its meanings in the worshippers' hearts. When music speaks to the listener, there is a response to the presence of God. A shifting takes place when the saints gather and actively participate in the encounter. This kind of shift will leave a residue of power where healing, miracles, signs, and wonders can be experienced.

Involving the chief worship leader

Even though the worship leader and the team have prepared sets for the encounter in advance, it is the chief worship leader who has the authority to obey God. If a shift needs to be made in the set, then the worship leader and the entire staff should adjust and obey God as well. To make the process easier, it is strongly recommended that the chief worship leader be included in the planning of songs and in what is going to be ministered during the encounter.

Creating effective song sets

If the chief worship leader is doing a series, it is highly recommended that songs be planned around the theme that will reinforce and set an atmosphere for miracles, signs, and wonders to happen. **If the chief is not doing a series, then it is recommended that the worship leader sing songs that speak to the current theme pattern that the chief is focusing on in that season. If neither is the case, then it is recommended that song sets are centered around the theme for the year or that song sets are familiar to the culture in the church.**

Thematic flow: In this flow, the worship leader plans songs around a theme that is either set by the chief worship leader or by the team itself. It is advised that, when planning thematic flows, the set flow with a familiar phrase, word, or thought. The medley should also include multigenerational and cultural styles.

Prophetic flow: As the worship leader plans to flow prophetically, there must be a connection with God. Then we wait for the spirit of God to speak a word that resonates with the flow of the moment, and we build on that word or phrase.

Rhythmic medley flow: As the worship leader plans sets for worship, the leader needs to be sure to avoid a major adjustment in the tempo of the song.

Song medleys: The beginning of the encounter should invite the worshippers to join in the celebratory ascension. Traditionally, the encounter begins with a solid strong upbeat song unless the atmosphere has been set by the chief worshipper or designee. If the atmosphere is set otherwise where there is a strong worship flow, then the worship leader should flow with the set tone of the house at the time and not try and force a shift.

Sample #1: ***Thematic/Contemporary***

How Great Is Our God
How Great Thou Art

Sample #2: ***Thematic***

Lord You Are Good and Your Mercy Endureth Forever
Lord You're Mighty
Lord I Love You

Sample #3: ***Traditional***

I Came to Magnify the Lord
I Love to Praise Him

Sample #4: ***Combination of Traditional and Contemporary***

Freedom
I'm Free Indeed
I am Free

Sample #5: ***Combination of Traditional and Contemporary***

Alpha and Omega
Holy, Holy, Holy
Total Praise

My takeaways

Tools that I will use

Notes

ABOUT THE AUTHOR

Bishop Michael A. Strickland is the proud son of the late Reverend Dr. Hopie Strickland, Jr. and Mrs. Linda D. Strickland. He is married to the former Brenda E. Clark and they are the parents of Briana Michelle, Morgan Lynn and Audria Hope Celeste. Affectionately called "Pastor Mike" or "Bishop" by the members of the Victory Tabernacle Church International, he serves faithfully and diligently in leading this congregation to become the church that God is pleased with and smiles upon. The vision that God has given him for the ministry is to "Expose God, Explore God's Word, and Exemplify God's character on earth."

Bishop Strickland received his undergraduate degree in Music Education from Valdosta State University in Valdosta, Georgia, a master's degree in Library Science from Jacksonville State University in Jacksonville, Alabama, and a master's degree in Biblical Studies from Beulah Heights University.

Bishop Strickland accepted his call to proclaim the Gospel of Jesus Christ in December 1995 and preached his initial sermon on the 4th Sunday in January, 1996. In 2000 he was called as pastor of the Little Bethel Baptist Church in Mableton, Georgia, and served there until 2004. After being led by the Lord to resign as pastor, Bishop Strickland was the "Joshua" assigned to serve as his father's assistant at Victory until his father's transition on July 12, 2007. On September 9, 2007, he became the pastor of the Victory Tabernacle Church.

He was elevated to the office of Bishop on July 12, 2009, by Bishop Ruth W. Smith, Presiding Prelate of the Light of the World International Interdenominational Association. He is proud of the fact that God has His hands in the plans for his life and submits himself completely to God's authority. He has done international ministry, preaching and ministering in London, England, as well as in Andobakedash and Chennai, India.

As a bi-vocational pastor, Bishop Strickland has been employed as a Music Specialist with the Atlanta Public Schools for more than 25 years. Two of his greatest honors are being twice named the "Teacher of the Year" and being highlighted in the Collegiate Edition of Outstanding Educators. As a gifted encourager, Bishop is known as the E3 guy: He will Empower, Encourage and Equip you to be the best you that you can be.

Bishop Strickland continues to grow in Christ: he enjoys worship, serving, preaching, singing, and empowering the people of God. All glory, honor, and praise belong to God, as the bishop continues to do what he loves doing—being who God would have him be.

www.ingramcontent.com/pod-product-compliance
Lightning Source LLC
LaVergne TN
LVHW061256100826
845148LV00008B/1146
* 9 7 8 1 7 3 7 4 4 2 2 0 2 *